Cold Feet

The city of Rosca is preparing for a presidential visit when the body of a young man is found near the American Consulate. He is very well-dressed, but there is something missing. Why isn't he wearing any shoes? It is Rymer's job to discover the man's identity. His investigation leads him to a theatre group with a very surprising final act.

....

Rod Smith is an experienced writer, teacher and musician. He writes novels and stories for people of all ages. He also writes music for film and television programmes. Rod was born in Oxford, England, but he now lives in Seville, southern Spain, with his wife and young son.

....
LEVEL THREE
....

Richmond Publishing
19 Berghem Mews
Blythe Road
London W14 OHN

© Rod Smith 1997
Published by Richmond Publishing® 1997
First published 1997

All rights reserved. No part of this book may be reproduced, stored in a retrieval system or transmitted in any form or by any means, electronic, mechanical, photocopying, recording or otherwise, without the prior permission of the publishers.

ISBN: 84-294-4921-3
Depósito legal: M-4851-2002
Printed in Spain by Palgraphi, S.A.

Cover Design: Giles Davies Design
Cover Illustration: Peter Sutton
Illustrations: Andy Walker

Cold Feet

ROD SMITH

RICHMOND READERS

LEVEL 1 (500 headwords)

Oscar   Jack's Game
Maria's Dilemma   Permission to Leave
The Boy from Yesterday

LEVEL 2 (800 headwords)

Saturday Storm   Craigen Castle Mystery
Jason Causes Chaos   Where's Mauriac?

LEVEL 3 (1200 headwords)

Cold Feet   A Christmas Carol
The Canterville Ghost and Other Stories
Dr Jekyll and Mr Hyde

LEVEL 4 (1800 headwords)

Dracula   Jane Eyre
The Adventures of Tom Sawyer
A Trip to London

PROLOGUE

The city of Rosca. Early morning: Monday, April 29th.

The cathedral clock was ten minutes slow. Carmen Viguera knew this so she didn't look up. She looked at her watch instead: 6.40 a.m. 'I'm ten minutes late,' she thought, as she hurried through the centre of the city.

She crossed *Plaza Mayor*. It was covered in flowers. They were there to welcome the president who was going to visit Rosca in a few days' time. But Carmen took no notice. She didn't like the president and she was late for work.

She ran down the Calle Alta ... and stopped in front of the side entrance.

She worked as a cleaner* in the U.S. consulate. It was a large, modern building on the far side of the square, opposite the Grand Hotel. She worked in the hotel, too, in the evenings. She had to: she had three small children and a husband who didn't earn much money.

She began to run. She ran down *Calle Alta*, a narrow street to the right of the consulate and stopped in front of the side entrance.

She looked up. The entrance was dark. She could only see the first step which led up to the door. She took a small torch from her pocket and turned it on.

A man was lying at the top of the steps. His eyes were open but he couldn't see anything.

He was dead.

The torch fell from Carmen's hand. She screamed.

Chapter 1
The Man with no Shoes

The phone rang in room 201 of the Grand Hotel. It rang five times, then stopped. The man in bed turned over and tried to go back to sleep.

The phone rang again. He picked it up and looked at his watch. It was seven o'clock.

'Rymer? Is that you?' It was a man's voice.

'Yes. Who is it?'

'It's Eliot. I'm phoning from the consulate.'

Eliot Lee was an American. He worked in the U.S. consulate and was a close friend of Rymer's.

'I hope it's important, Eliot. I was asleep.'

'What about murder?'

'Murder? In the consulate?' Someone moved in the room next door and Rymer lowered* his voice. 'What's happened exactly?'

'I arrived at work early this morning, around six thirty - there's a lot to do before the president arrives. I'd been here about fifteen minutes when I heard a scream. It came from the side entrance. I went to the door. The first thing I saw when I opened it was Carmen Viguera, one of our cleaners. She was crying. Then I found out why. There was a dead man lying at the side of the doorway.'

'Do you have any idea how long he'd been there?'

'No. I imagine he was there before I arrived. But I can't be sure. I never use the side entrance. I always come in the front way.'

'Uh-huh. Have you called the police?'

7

'No, not yet. I, uh, wanted to speak to you first.'

'Why?'

'Well the situation is difficult. We Americans are very unpopular. You see, six months ago the FBI shot and killed a man in Miami. His name was Carlos Barreda, and he came from Rosca. Although he was a criminal, he had a lot of influence here. He regularly gave money to the poor, and for this reason many people respected him. After his death there was a lot of anti-American feeling. This has made things very difficult for us. Recently the situation has improved, but relations with the local authorities are still not good.'

'Is that why you don't want to call the police?'

'Yes, not immediately anyway. I'll have to contact them soon, of course. But I don't think they will try very hard to discover who killed this man. They might want people to think that we are responsible. The president arrives in a few days' time. The publicity could be very bad for us. The authorities here could even use this death as an excuse to close the consulate. My government wouldn't like that, Rymer. That's why I wanted to speak to you first. I need you to find out the truth before the president arrives.'

'But I'm on holiday, Eliot. It was your suggestion, remember? "Come and enjoy the celebrations. Bring your camera. You'll get some great pictures." Those were your exact words.'

'I know, I know. But my job could depend on this, Rymer. And you're the only person who can help me. You see, it's easier for you: you're English, not American. And people know that. They know you, too. Many of them still remember your father because of the work he did here with the Red Cross. But they don't know that you're a private investigator. They don't know you're an old friend of mine, either.'

Rymer tried to sound enthusiastic. 'OK. I'll get dressed. Give me ten minutes.'

■ ■ ■

It was 7.20 a.m. when Rymer arrived at the consulate. He followed Eliot to the side entrance. The two men stood in the doorway, looking down at the body.

The two men stood in the doorway, looking down at the body.

It was the body of a young man. He looked foreign. He had blue eyes, brown hair and pale skin. The eyes were open and the expression on the man's face was calm. He wore a dark blue jacket, grey trousers, a white shirt and a red tie. The clothes looked expensive and they fitted him perfectly. In fact, everything about his appearance was perfect.

Except for one thing. He wore no shoes.

'Why do you think he was murdered?' Rymer asked.

'His death is suspicious for a number of reasons,' Eliot replied. 'The first thing I noticed – like you, I imagine – is the fact that he's not wearing any shoes. Then I checked his clothes. All the pockets are empty: no identification, no money, no keys – nothing. There is no sign of violence, either. So I don't think anything was taken by force. And how did he die? Did he kill himself by taking drugs? If so, why would he empty his pockets and take off his shoes? It doesn't make sense. Murder is the only thing that does make sense.'

Rymer agreed but he said nothing. He pulled out a small automatic camera and photographed the dead man's face. Then he took out the film and gave it to Eliot. 'Can you get this developed for me – quickly?'

'It might take a couple of hours.'

'That's OK. Look, maybe you should go and phone the police now. How long do you think it'll take them to arrive?'

'Five, ten minutes?'

'Fine. That's all the time I need.'

Eliot left, wondering what his friend was going to do.

Rymer worked quickly: it was getting lighter now and people would soon be coming down the street.

THE MAN WITH NO SHOES

First he examined the dead man's clothes. He noticed that there were no labels* on any of the clothing. This was strange. And when he checked the man's pockets he found something even stranger: a small, soft object in the top outside pocket of the dead man's jacket. So, Eliot had missed something. Rymer pulled it out.

It was a small, round capsule*. He held it up to the light. It was full of liquid. What could it be? Some kind of drug which the man needed? Was it used to kill him?

Rymer imagined a possible situation:

Someone decides to kill a man. He knows that this man takes capsules containing a drug which is dangerous in large amounts. One day, possibly while his victim is sleeping, the murderer takes the capsules from the man's jacket pocket. He puts a fatal quantity inside something which will hide the taste of the drug - a bottle of whisky, perhaps? Later, he offers the man a drink. The man accepts, thinking it comes from a friend. A short while later, he's dead.*

Is this what happened? If so, the murderer wasn't very careful. He left one of the capsules in the dead man's pocket.

But this was just an idea. And probably not a very good one, because it didn't explain why the victim was wearing socks*, but no shoes.

Rymer felt the man's feet. They were cold. How long had he been dead? Four hours? At least that, but probably no more than five, otherwise someone would have seen him. He looked closely at the dead man's socks. They were pulled towards his heels* and some tiny stones were caught in the material. This showed that he had been walking before he died. But not far, and not for very long: the stones were the same as those in the area, and the socks were still in good condition.

Rymer stood up. It was important to find out what the capsule contained. Maybe Eliot could get someone to do an analysis. He put the capsule in his pocket and went back into the consulate.

As Rymer left, a man moved from the shadows* on the opposite side of the street. He was a large man with small eyes and a brutal face. He walked away, quickly, and went to a phone booth* in *Plaza Mayor*. After a short conversation he left the booth and crossed the square. When he reached the other side he stopped and looked at a small metal object he was carrying in his right hand. He smiled.

It was a key: the key to room 201 of the Grand Hotel.

Chapter 2
The Attack in Room 201

When the police arrived, Eliot immediately took them to where the body was found. Rymer went with him.

A small crowd were standing around the side entrance to the consulate. Two of the policemen pushed them back. Another policeman – a thin, unfriendly man in a grey suit – began talking to Eliot.

An ambulance arrived. Rymer looked at his watch. It was ten minutes to eight – time to leave.

He pushed through the crowd and began walking back to the hotel. It was light now but the air was still cool. At the top of *Calle Alta* he smelt coffee and looked over to the left. On the corner of the street was *Los Pinos*, the oldest café in Rosca. Its doors were open and the lights inside looked warm and inviting. And yet the place was empty.

'Most of the people who use it are probably standing outside the consulate,' thought Rymer.

Most, but not all, he suddenly realised.

A girl was looking out of one of the windows. She had long, red hair and a face he could fall in love with: beautiful, mysterious, and sad. Their eyes met and she turned away.

A girl was looking out of one of the windows.

COLD FEET

Rymer crossed *Plaza Mayor*, thinking about the girl. She looked foreign, a little lost. He was curious. Where was she from? What was she doing in Rosca? And why was she sitting alone, looking so sad? He tried to forget these questions. The answers might be interesting but he had neither the time nor the opportunity to think about them now.

Forget about the girl and concentrate on the case, he told himself.

■ ■ ■

News of suspicious death travels fast. Most of the staff* of the Grand Hotel were standing at the main entrance, talking about what had happened.

Rymer went to the reception desk to collect his key. There was no one there.

'Excuse me?' The words were English, but the voice sounded foreign.

He turned. An old lady stood in front of him. She was tall, thin, and aristocratic. 'You're British, aren't you?' she asked.

Rymer looked surprised. 'That's right. How did you know?'

'Last night I heard you talking to Luis, the receptionist, in English.' She lowered her voice. 'His pronunciation is terrible.'

Rymer laughed. 'Yes, but he likes to practise.'

The old lady smiled back at him. Rymer noticed she was carrying a German magazine. It was unusual to meet other Europeans in this part of the world. It was even more unusual to meet ones you liked.

'My name's Rymer,' he said, offering his hand.

THE ATTACK IN ROOM 201

An old lady stood in front of him. She was tall, thin and aristocratic.

'Is that your first name?'

'No. Everyone calls me by my surname. I don't like my first name.'

'Then I won't ask you what it is,' said the old lady. Still smiling, she took his hand. 'My name is Mrs. Strelski. Imra Strelski.'

'Are you with your husband?'

She looked suddenly sad. 'Oh no,' she said. 'My husband died a long time ago.' There was a pause. '1968. In Czechoslovakia. When the Russians …'

'I'm sorry,' said Rymer, quickly.

She changed the subject. 'I came down for breakfast, but there was no one in the restaurant. I wanted to ask Luis what was happening. But one of the other employees* said something to him and he went away in a hurry. Now everyone is standing by the main entrance. They seem very interested in the buildings on the other side of *Plaza Mayor*. Has anything happened?'

Rymer looked serious. 'Someone found a dead man at the side entrance to the U.S. consulate. His death looks suspicious. It could be murder.'

'Oh, how awful.' She turned pale.

Rymer was afraid she was going to fall. Gently, he led her to a chair by the reception desk. 'Would you like a glass of water?' he asked.

She smiled, weakly. 'How very kind of you.'

Rymer went to get a glass of water from the hotel bar. There was another customer there, a young man who looked like a typical worker from Rosca. He also looked bored. That wasn't surprising. There was no one to serve him: the barman, like the rest of the staff, was standing at

THE ATTACK IN ROOM 201

the main entrance.

'Good morning,' said Rymer.

The man didn't answer. He gave Rymer an unfriendly look and left the room.

Strange person, thought Rymer. He took a glass from behind the bar and filled it with water.

Back at reception he gave Mrs. Strelski the glass. As she took it he noticed that her hands were trembling*.

She drank quickly, then looked up. 'You must excuse me,' she said. 'News of violence always upsets me.'

'I understand,' said Rymer. 'There's no need to apologise.'

She stood up and smiled. 'Let's go to the restaurant. We can have a cup of tea together. And if there's no one there ...' she paused, 'we can serve ourselves.'

■ ■ ■

Twenty minutes later Rymer was standing at reception once again. His conversation with Mrs. Strelski had been interesting. She had told him that she lived with her daughter in Buenos Aires. She had moved there following her husband's death in 1968. She was now travelling around South America for three months, alone.

Rymer thought about the old lady. She seemed interested in him. Maybe this was because she was lonely and needed someone to talk to. Oh well, it didn't really matter. She was good company. And he admired her. An old lady travelling around South America on her own ....

He looked at his watch. It was almost ten o'clock. He was about to get the key to his room from behind the reception desk when Luis came back.

'I am so sorry,' said the receptionist. He was a short,

dark man with a loud voice who was always looking for an excuse to talk.

'That's OK. Room 201, please.'

'Of course, Mr Rymer,' said Luis, as he turned to get the key. 'And a very good morning to you, sir.' His smile looked false and his manner was too polite. He didn't give Rymer the key, but began asking questions without waiting for a reply. 'And how are we today? Fine? Good, good.'

Rymer didn't have time to talk. He took the key from Luis's hand, smiled, and walked away. He decided to take the stairs to the second floor. The lift was too close to the reception desk.

When Rymer walked into his room he sensed that he was not alone. He turned. Too late. Something hard hit him on the side of the head and he fell to the ground. He felt someone pulling things from his pockets, then move away. He looked up. A large, heavy man was climbing out of the window on the other side of the room.

Rymer stood up, slowly. His head hurt and his legs felt weak. He went to the window and looked below. A man was running down the fire escape*. Rymer didn't try to catch him. He watched as the man got into a new Mercedes, parked on the opposite side of the street, and drove away. He noted the number, went back into the room and wrote it down.

He sat on the edge of the bed. He felt sick and his head ached. The contents of his pockets were lying by the door. He was surprised to see his wallet among them. He was even more surprised when he looked inside. His

THE ATTACK IN ROOM 201

A man was running down the fire escape.

money was still there. How strange. What had the man taken?

He put everything on the bed. Nothing was missing. He put the wallet back in the pocket of his jacket. The pocket felt wet. He wondered why. And then he knew. Of course, the capsule. It broke when he fell and the liquid came out. But there was no sign of the capsule itself. It was missing.

This meant two things: there was a connection between the attack and the dead man; and the capsule was important.

He phoned the consulate. The receptionist told him that Eliot was still with the police. He left a message asking for him to call back as soon as he was free.

He closed the window and locked it again. There was no way anyone could get in from the outside unless they broke the glass. And the glass wasn't broken. So how did the man get into the room? With a key to the main door? But the key had been in reception. It didn't make sense.

The phone rang.

'Rymer?'

'Hello, Eliot.'

'They gave me your message.'

'Good. Look, I've just been attacked.'

'What? Are you all right?'

'No, but I'm getting better – slowly.'

'Who was it? Where did it happen?'

'It happened here, in my room. I don't know who it was but I saw his car. It was a new Mercedes. I wrote down the number. Do you think you can find out the name of the owner?'

'If it's a local number I can probably get the information

THE ATTACK IN ROOM 201

from the place that sold it.'

'Good.' Rymer gave him the number. 'Can you do that as soon as possible?'

'Of course. Did you lose much money?'

'None. He took something more significant. It has a connection with the dead man.'

Eliot waited for Rymer to explain.

'It's a small capsule. I found it on the body. I didn't want to tell you about it while the police were there. The thing is,' Rymer continued, 'when I fell, the capsule broke and the liquid went into my jacket pocket. I'd like to find out what it is, if possible.'

'I'll get someone to do an analysis. Stay in the hotel if you're not feeling well. I'll come and collect the jacket.'

'No, don't do that. I'll take a shower then bring it round myself. I need some fresh air.'

'All right. Look, are you sure you're OK?' Eliot sounded worried. *'I think you should see a doctor. Let me get one for you.'*

'No, no, that won't be necessary. I'll be all right. I'll see you in a while.'

■ ■ ■

Half an hour later Rymer arrived at the consulate. The receptionist looked up as he entered the building. 'Ah, Mr. Rymer,' she said. 'Eliot's not here at the moment, I'm afraid. He left this for you.' She gave him a small suitcase.

Rymer opened the case. Inside there was a note, a set of car keys, and a gun. He picked up the gun. It was loaded*. Carefully, he put it in the pocket of the coat he was wearing. Then he read the note:

> Rymer
>
> Sorry I can't see you at the moment – I have to go to the police station. I'll be back around 4 p.m. Name and address of the owner of the car is: Juan Aguado, Villa Rosa, C/General Sanz, 99. Rosca.
> Aguado is a private investigator. The police suspect that he works with criminals, although he's never been caught – he's too careful for that.
> If you don't want to wait for me and prefer to see him alone, use my car.
> The gun is an extra precaution. Please take care.
>
> Eliot
>
> P.S. Put your jacket in the suitcase and leave it with the receptionist.

Chapter 3
Another Murder

General Sanz was a beautiful street on the west side of the city. It was a nice place to live – if you had the money.

Villa Rosa was the last house on the left. Rymer drove slowly past the entrance and parked around the corner.

He walked back to the house. The Mercedes stood in the driveway: Aguado was at home.

ANOTHER MURDER

He looked up at *Villa Rosa*. It didn't look like the home of a violent* man. It had a red roof*, white walls and a wooden* balcony covered in flowers. It was an attractive place: romantic, colourful and quiet. Too quiet. There was something else, too: the shutters* on all the windows were closed – strange for mid afternoon.

He looked up at Villa Rosa. It didn't look like the home of a violent man.

COLD FEET

He went to the front door and knocked. The door opened slightly. He moved back in surprise, then knocked again. No reply. He stood there, listening. Not a sound came from inside. Maybe Aguado was in the back garden? He went to look. But there was no back garden, only a small patio area. And Aguado wasn't there.

He went back to the front door and stepped inside the house. There were stairs leading to the first floor. As he looked up a sudden rush* of wind closed the door behind him. He stood in the darkness, listening. He could hear a clock, at the far end of the hall. It made him feel nervous, as if the house were alive. He found a door to his right, pushed it open and stepped into a large room. There was a strange smell in the air: a mixture of heat, alcohol, perfume and smoke. He turned on the light.

Aguado sat in front of him. An empty bottle of whisky and two small glasses lay on the floor, near his feet. His eyes were open and there was a large red hole at the top of his head. The face beneath it was covered in blood.

Aguado was dead. He'd been shot.

Rymer checked Aguado's clothes. He found a wallet, full of banknotes*, in the inside pocket of his jacket. Obviously, whoever killed him wasn't interested in his money. There were also two cards in the wallet. Rymer pulled them out. One was a driving permit*, the other was a licence to work as a private investigator. There was no sign of the capsule. That didn't really matter, Rymer realised. The analysis of his jacket would soon tell him what the capsule contained.

He put back the wallet and turned to search the room.

Suddenly he froze. He could hear footsteps. They were coming towards the house. He hid behind the door and waited, his heart beating fast.

The footsteps stopped. He heard the front door move, followed by the sound of paper landing on the hall floor. There was a brief silence. The footsteps started again, then disappeared.

Rymer looked out into the hall. Three letters lay at the bottom of the stairs. He relaxed. It was only the postman. But someone else might come at any minute. It was time to get out of the place – quickly.

He left the house by the front door and walked back down the garden path. Before entering the street he checked to see if anyone was there. The street was empty. Good – no one had noticed him. He walked quickly back to the car.

Two questions filled Rymer's head as he drove back to the city: Why had Aguado been killed? And what was he, Rymer, going to do about it?

Finding an answer to the first question would be difficult. He began by going over his ideas on the case so far.

Sometime during the night, a man dies in suspicious circumstances. It looks like murder, with a drug overdose* as the probable cause of death. It seems probable, too, that the drugs are taken at a place which is not far from the U.S. consulate. Of course, the man takes them without realising: (maybe he accepts a drink from someone whom he thinks is a friend). Feeling the effects of the drugs, he walks off and collapses at the side entrance to the consulate. The murderer follows. He watches, *and waits. Finally, when he is sure that the man is dead, he goes up to the body. He then removes* anything which could identify his victim, including the man's shoes, and leaves.*

So what was Aguado's connection with these possible events?

Aguado, like Rymer, was a private investigator. But, unlike Rymer, he had worked with criminals. The murderer knew this. So he employed Aguado to stop anyone discovering how the man with no shoes had died. This is why Aguado attacked Rymer and then took the capsule.

But how did Aguado know about it? Rymer had told no one, not even Eliot, about the capsule. And yet Aguado knew exactly where it was. This could only mean one thing: he had seen Rymer put it in his pocket. A short while later, Aguado got into room 201. How? Probably by taking the key while Luis was away from reception. But the key was there when Rymer got back to the hotel, a few minutes later. Did Aguado somehow return the key? That was impossible, surely?

As Rymer thought about Aguado's connection with the case he realised how little he really knew. In fact, he was certain of only one thing: that it was Aguado who took the capsule.

And now he was dead. Why?

There was a large amount of money in Aguado's wallet. Had Aguado asked for even more money? Was the murderer afraid that Aguado would still talk? There had been no sign of a fight. Did this mean that the murderer had agreed to pay? Again, Rymer imagined a possible situation:

Aguado takes the money, feeling pleased with himself. He

returns the capsule to his employer and suggests that they have a drink to celebrate the end of their business. The murderer smiles, and accepts. Aguado lowers his head to pour out the whisky. The murderer pulls out a gun and shoots him dead.

Rymer was reasonably satisfied with this analysis; but as he reached the city centre the second question became more immediately important. What should he do about Aguado's death? Should he tell the police, or keep quiet? Either way it would be better to speak to Eliot first.

He looked at his watch: ten to four. At four o'clock he would go back to the consulate.

He parked the car in *Plaza Mayor*, and waited.

■ ■ ■

A few metres from where Rymer sat, a young woman was looking into a mirror. She didn't like what she saw. She turned away and lit a cigarette. Through an open door on the far side of the room came the sound of running water. And then a voice, cold and determined.

'In twenty-four hours we will be safe, Katrina. Rymer is our only problem. But not for long. I will lead him to us. And then ... ? I will kill him. Only two things are important: remember how much I love you, and do exactly as I say.'

I love you. Katrina shivered. She felt sick and frightened.

The sound of water grew louder. The person whose love she didn't want was taking a shower.

Katrina put down her cigarette. As she did so, something in the mirror caught her attention. There was a small black case under the bed. She hadn't noticed it before. Carefully, she pulled it out and opened it.

COLD FEET

Inside the case was a gun. It was covered with a white cloth. Under the cloth was a letter.

Inside the case was a gun. It was covered with a white cloth. Under the cloth was a letter. Katrina took it out, began to read, then stopped. There was a curious expression on her face. Slowly, she walked over to the window and held the letter up to the light. Seconds later, her face turned a deep, burning red.

The same colour as her hair.

Chapter 4
Back in the Consulate

'What I don't understand,' Eliot said, 'is how Aguado knew so much about you. He knew you were working on the case. He knew you were staying at the Grand Hotel. He even knew the number of your room.'

'He also knew about the capsule,' said Rymer. 'Have you found out what it contained?'

'No. And that's another strange thing. According to the police, the man died of barbiturate "poisoning". But, so far, our tests on the capsule haven't identified barbiturates – nor any other kind of drug or poison.'

'You'll have to keep trying,' Rymer said, surprised by the news. He returned to the previous subject. 'I'm thinking about Aguado again. If he saw me find the capsule, it means he was hiding somewhere near the consulate before I arrived.'

'I imagine he hid in one of the doorways on the opposite side of the street. He had probably been there for hours.'

'I don't think so. Why did Aguado need to stand and watch what happened to the body? The murderer had almost nothing to fear from the police.'

'Why do you say that?' asked Eliot.

'The dead man looked foreign. The police don't usually spend much time investigating the death of an unidentified foreigner. There's another thing too: the murderer probably knew about the bad relations between you and the people of the city. The man's death won't make things any easier. An unexplained murder on the steps of the consulate is just what the authorities need if

29

they want to close it down. The murderer knew that. It gave him an almost perfect situation in which to commit the crime.'

'So why did he employ Aguado?'

'I can think of two reasons. First, the murderer was worried when he found out I was investigating the crime, so he told Aguado to follow me. Second, he realised that he'd left one of the capsules on the body: Aguado was sent to get it back. But we got there first.'

Eliot thought for a moment. 'Either way, they knew a lot about you,' he said. 'And I don't understand how. I called you at seven o'clock this morning. Twenty minutes later we were examining the dead man. In that short space of time the murderer did several things. He found out that you were investigating the crime and he discovered where you were staying. He also had enough time to contact Aguado and tell him to get to the scene of the crime before us. But it takes longer than twenty minutes to get from Aguado's house to the centre of town. It doesn't make sense.'

'No, it doesn't. But one thing is obvious.'

'What's that?'

'The murderer heard our telephone conversation. Either at the hotel, or here – in the consulate.'

Eliot looked surprised.

'Who was in the consulate when you called me?' Rymer asked.

'Only myself and Carmen Viguera, the lady who found the body.'

'Are you sure about that?'

'Absolutely.'

'What about when you called me at the hotel? Who

answered the phone?'

'A man. I don't know who it was. He connected the call to your room.'

'Luis,' said Rymer, angrily.

'Who?'

'Luis – the hotel receptionist. If he listened to our conversation half of Rosca would know the details within about ten minutes.'

Eliot laughed. 'I know the type,' he said. 'But even if he did hear my news, who could he tell at that time of the day?'

'The hotel staff, other guests – if any of them were up that early. The hotel bar opens at seven o'clock, before any of the city's cafés, so quite a lot of people go for a coffee there. Perhaps the murderer was among them.'

'But that still doesn't explain how Aguado was able to arrive at the scene so quickly.'

'No, unless …' Rymer thought for a moment. 'Imagine this situation. The murderer commits a very clever crime. He feels sure that no one will discover either the identity of his victim, or how and why he died. This makes him feel proud*. But he feels something else, too.'

'What's that?'

'Curiosity. He wants to know what will happen when the body is found. But he doesn't want to return to the scene of the crime. So he employs Aguado to be his eyes. He wants Aguado to be in the area when the body is found. He also wants him to act if anything unexpected happens.'

'And something unexpected did happen. When I asked you to investigate the crime. And then when you found the capsule.'

'Exactly. Anyway, I imagine that the murderer had booked Aguado into the same hotel as me, probably using a different name. And then what happens is this: shortly after you phone me at the hotel, the murderer finds out that I will be investigating the death of the man with no shoes. He tells Aguado to wait around the reception area until I come down, then follow me. A few minutes later, I arrive. Luis is not at reception. I leave my key on the desk and go to the consulate. Aguado takes the key and follows. He sees me find the capsule. He realises that the capsule is important, returns to the hotel before I do and, using the key, gets into my room. When I walk in he attacks me, takes the capsule and goes back to *Villa Rosa*, where he lives.'

There was a pause. 'The only mystery,' said Eliot, 'is how did Aguado return the key to reception? Because it was there when you got back to the hotel.'

'I know,' said Rymer. 'But maybe I'll find an answer to that problem later. At the moment, let's concentrate on what Aguado does next. I think he calls the murderer from *Villa Rosa* and tells him about the capsule. A short time later the murderer comes to collect it. Before returning the capsule, Aguado asks for more money. Result? He gets shot.'

'And that's what you think happened?'

'Yes. But it's only an idea. I could be wrong. And it doesn't explain the murder of the unidentified man.'

'So what are you going to do next?'

'I was hoping you would tell me.'

'Oh?'

'Yes. Should I tell the police about Aguado's death? Or say nothing?'

Eliot thought for a moment. 'Did anyone see you?'

'I don't think so.'

'Then it's better to keep quiet about it. The police will find out soon enough. Here ...' Eliot took an envelope from his jacket pocket and gave it to Rymer. 'These are the photos you asked to have developed. What are you going to do with them?'

'I'll show them to the owners of the shops and bars around the centre. Someone might recognise the man's face.'

'Are you going to talk to Luis?'

Eliot took an envelope from his jacket pocket and gave it to Rymer. 'These are the photos you asked to have developed.'

'I suppose so. But I don't think he'll tell me the truth.'
'Well, try anyway. And good luck.'

Rymer didn't feel lucky. He gave a weak smile and left the building.

■ ■ ■

'Tonight we leave for the capital. We will kill Rymer there.'

The words were like a knife through Katrina's heart.

'Why are you so sure that he'll go to the capital?' she asked.

'I told you. Rymer is a clever man. He knows about that fool, Aguado. And very soon he'll find out how Czerny died.'

'Paul ...,' said Katrina. She spoke softly and tears came to her eyes.

'Don't cry, Katrina.' Cold, dry fingers touched the girl's face. 'Stay with me and you'll be all right. Leave, and you'll be sorry. But you wouldn't do that, would you?'

Katrina couldn't answer.

Chapter 5
The Clue in Calle Alta

By early evening Rymer was back at the hotel. He went to the bar, ordered a drink and sat down at one of the tables. He was in a bad mood. He had spent three hours enquiring in local shops and bars with no result. And the city's bus and taxi drivers hadn't helped, either. No one had recognised the dead man. And no one had seen or heard anything unusual on the night he died.

His conversation with Luis had been just as disappointing. Luis said he had seen no one looking like Aguado in the hotel that morning. As far as he knew, no one of that description was staying there. He had heard about the murder outside the consulate from one of the other employees. And then Rymer remembered something Mrs. Strelski had said: 'I wanted to ask Luis what was happening. But one of the other employees said something to him and he went away in a hurry.'

It seemed that Luis was telling the truth. And that was worrying. Because if Luis hadn't heard the telephone conversation between Eliot and Rymer, who had?

Just then the door opened and Mrs. Strelski came into the room. She was walking with difficulty.

'Come and join me,' Rymer said. He felt in need of a friend. He stood up and helped her across the room.

'Thank you. You're very kind. My legs are not as young as they were.'

But your eyes are, Rymer thought. Those eyes clearly didn't miss very much. And then an idea occurred to him. Mrs. Strelski had been up early that morning. Perhaps she had seen something. He would ask her. But first, a social question. 'What would you like to drink?'

'A gin and tonic, please. Thank you.'

She sat down. Rymer ordered two drinks. As they were waiting for them to arrive he noticed that Mrs. Strelski was looking at him with a worried expression on her face.

Moments later, he found out why. 'I heard that you were attacked by a thief. In your room, Luis said. I'm so sorry. Were you hurt?'

'A little. Not too badly.'

'Oh, that's good, did you lose much money?'

'None, fortunately.' He decided not to mention the capsule. He didn't want to worry the old lady. But it was a good time to ask if she had seen anything.

'Mrs. Strelski,' he said. 'You were up early this morning. Can you remember who was in the reception area when you came down for breakfast?'

'No, not really. I went straight to the restaurant, you see. When I saw that it was empty, I went to reception. But before I reached the desk, Luis left with another member of staff.'

'And there was no one else around?'

She thought for a moment. 'Not at reception, no. But I did see a man going into the bar. That was just before you arrived.'

Rymer remembered the unfriendly man he met when he went to get Mrs. Strelski a glass of water. He had forgotten about him until now.

'What did he look like, do you remember?'

'Oh let's see ...' she paused. 'Nothing special, really. Medium-height, difficult to tell his age. I don't know, just very ordinary-looking if you know what I mean.'

Rymer was sure it was the same one. 'Do you know if he's staying in the hotel?' he asked.

'I think he left earlier – I heard him asking one of the staff about hotels in the capital. But I'm sure he was staying here. I met him yesterday morning, too. In the restaurant. We were the only ones there. I didn't speak to him. He didn't look very friendly.'

Rymer was disappointed. The man probably had nothing to do with the case, but his unfriendly behaviour was a little strange. If he was still in the hotel Rymer could ask him some questions. There was no chance of that now – the man had gone.

They fell silent. Mrs. Strelski lifted her glass. Once again, Rymer noticed her trembling hands.

'Do you always get up early?' he asked.

'Yes. I don't sleep as well as I used to. The slightest sound wakes me: a passing car, the cry of a bird, a distant telephone.'

'I'm sorry.'

'Oh, there's no need to be sorry. After all, getting up early gives me the chance to see something wonderful every day.'

'Oh? And what's that?'

'The sun coming up,' she said, gently. 'Sunrise* – so much more beautiful than sunset*. The first brings light, the second only darkness.'

There was sadness in her voice. Rymer thought he knew what caused it: loneliness, and the fear of growing old. He tried to talk about lighter things but was depressed by the day's events. And the alcohol didn't help. Perhaps a walk in the fresh air would do him good.

He put down his glass, made his excuses, and left the hotel.

■ ■ ■

The centre was quiet. Most people were staying at home, saving their money for the president's visit. He was going to arrive the following Friday. This was also the first day of a local festival, so celebrations would last all night long.

Even the cafés and bars were closing early, Rymer

COLD FEET

Even the cafés and bars were closing early, Rymer noticed. The only place open was a cinema, the Rialto.

THE CLUE IN CALLE ALTA

noticed. The only place open was a cinema, the *Rialto*.

It stood to the right of *Los Pinos*, its entrance – like the Town Hall – bright with coloured lights. The lights hurt his eyes. He turned away and thought about his conversation with Mrs. Strelski.

He remembered what she had said about the man in the bar. He, too, liked getting up early. He was certainly around at the time Rymer was attacked.

But lots of people like getting up early, Rymer told himself. The only strange thing about the man was his manner. And that wasn't enough to suspect him of murder.

But there was something else Mrs. Strelski had said, too. Something important. He tried to identify what it was, but he was finding it increasingly difficult to concentrate.

He stopped thinking and began to walk.

A few minutes later, he was standing at the top of *Calle Alta*. The street descended slightly and turned off to the right. He looked down the hill and tried to imagine what had happened the previous night.

Why was the dead man lying outside the consulate? How had he got there? Why was he not wearing any shoes? And where were those shoes now? Rymer remembered two things about the man's socks: they were pulled towards his heels, and they were in good condition. From this he made two conclusions: the man had walked down the hill, not up, and he had not walked very far. But where had he come from?

Rymer looked at the buildings to his right. At the top of the street was the café, Los Pinos. Next to this was a photography shop, then a travel agency followed by the long back wall of a car park.

Earlier that afternoon he had checked in the café and with the owners of the shops. No one knew anything about the dead man. But he hadn't looked closely at the buildings themselves. He did so now.

The first thing he noticed was that the travel agency had a deep entrance. It was a good place to hide. He was sure that Aguado had watched him from there. But the dead man? Had he come from one of these buildings? Rymer didn't think so. From where then? Certainly not from a bus or taxi, someone might have recognised him. And private cars were not allowed in the centre.

It didn't make any sense. In fact, nothing made any sense. There were no suspects, no useful information, and no obvious motive* for the crime. Quite simply, it was as if a stranger had appeared from nowhere without being seen or heard by anyone. It was a total mystery.

And yet Rymer had a feeling that the answer to the mystery lay in front of him. There was an important clue*, somewhere in that street. If only he knew where to look and what he was looking for. But he didn't. He was getting nowhere. He almost wanted to give up.

He looked down the street for one last time. Everything was dark, empty, and silent.

Or was it? And as Rymer asked himself that question he heard a sound: a low, beating sound which came from somewhere to the right. It sounded like an underground train.

But it was not a train. It was the answer to a mystery.

Chapter 6
The Green Door

The sound grew louder. Rymer saw a door open. From behind it, a crowd of laughing teenagers* ran into the street. He watched them go towards *Plaza Mayor*, where they stood waiting for a bus.

When the street was empty again, Rymer went to look at the door. It was in the middle of the car park wall and was painted the same colour – dark green. This made it difficult to see. Even so, Rymer was angry that he didn't look more carefully before.

It was clear what the door was used for: it was the side exit* to the *Rialto* cinema whose main entrance was in *Plaza Mayor*. This fact opened up a number of interesting possibilities which gave him some new ideas on the case. He thought about these and began to imagine the events of the previous night in a different way:

... it was the side exit to the Rialto *cinema.*

COLD FEET

A man goes with a 'friend' to see a late-night film. There are not many people in the cinema, so the man relaxes by kicking off his shoes and putting his feet over the seat in front. The 'friend' goes to buy a couple of drinks. He buys the drinks, puts a deadly quantity of barbiturates into one of them, comes back and gives it to his victim. Soon after drinking, the victim begins to feel very strange. All he wants to do is to get outside, quickly. He can't wait to put on his shoes and leaves the cinema by the side exit. He walks a little way down Calle Alta and collapses at the side entrance to the consulate. A short while later, he dies. When the film has ended, or possibly before, the murderer picks up the man's shoes and takes them away. Later, when no one is around, he goes to Calle Alta and makes sure that nothing is left on the dead man's body which could identify who he is.

But what about the other people leaving the cinema? Would they not have noticed the man lying in the consulate doorway? Not necessarily. When the man was found he had not been dead for more than a few hours. This meant he had probably been watching a late night film, one that finished around two, or even three, a.m. At that time the street would be very dark – the lights in *Plaza Mayor* were turned off shortly after midnight. And even if anyone did notice a man lying in the consulate doorway they would probably think he was sleeping off the effects of too much alcohol.

So was that the answer? Did that explain where the man had come from and why he had not been wearing any shoes? It seemed the most likely explanation, although there was still the problem of the capsule to consider.

A small detail, he told himself, and went back to the hotel in a far better mood.

42

Luis stood behind the reception desk, drinking coffee. He saw Rymer approach and put the cup down, guiltily. The air smelt slightly of brandy.

'Good evening, sir.' The false white smile appeared as if by magic. 'I think you have your key.'

'That's right, I do.' Rymer stood for a moment.

'Uh, ... do you want something else?'

'Yesterday's newspaper, if possible. Do you have it?'

Luis relaxed. He reached under the desk. 'No problem.' He gave Rymer a large newspaper. Rymer opened it. The films were listed in the middle pages, beneath the names of the cinemas where they were shown. Silently, Rymer read out the names to himself: *Astoria, Florida, Mirador, Victoria*? Where was the *Rialto*? He went through the names again, more slowly this time. There was no mistake. The *Rialto* wasn't listed.

Luis interrupted his thoughts. 'You are looking for something ... special, sir?'

'Yes. I wanted to know what was on at the *Rialto* last night. For some reason it's not listed.'

'I am sorry, sir, but that cinema is closed on Sundays.'

'Closed? Are you sure?'

'Yes, sir.'

Rymer felt a stab* of disappointment. He gave back the newspaper, wondering what to do next. If the cinema was closed he was back where he started – unless they'd been showing a private film. It wasn't much to hope for but he should at least go and check.

■ ■ ■

It was just after ten when he arrived at the *Rialto*. The film had just started. It was called *Death Of A President*. It seemed like a bad choice.

A fat man with a flowery shirt stood in the ticket office. He was reading a book. He sensed, rather than saw Rymer approach and automatically laid a ticket on the counter.

When no attempt was made to take it the man looked up.

'Can I help you?' he asked.

Rymer was surprised. He hadn't expected to be spoken to in English.

The man laughed. 'My name is Raúl. I am the owner of this ...' he looked around, proudly, '... palacio.' He moved his head forward, as if wishing to share a secret. 'My wife,' he said. 'She is from Scotland. She teaches English. I was one of her first students. That's how we met.' He smiled, a romantic look in his eyes. Rymer was about to ask an obvious question when Raúl saved him the trouble. 'I was in *Los Pinos* this afternoon. I heard you asking about the poor man found at the consulate. I knew then that you were English.'

'Oh. How?'

'From your manner, sir. My wife says that you can always tell an intelligent Englishman – they pretend to be shy. It gives them time to think.'

'Interesting,' said Rymer. He didn't know whether to be pleased or upset.

'Do you want to see the film? It's not very good.'

'Uh ... no, thank you,' said Rymer. He admired the man's honesty. 'I just wanted to know if any films were shown yesterday. You know, a private club, or something similar.'

Raúl shook his head. 'No, I am afraid not. There are

no films on Sundays. The cinema is closed.'

Rymer had expected this reply, but he was still disappointed. His ideas about the man's death were now useless. 'Ah well,' he said. 'Thanks anyway.' He gave a weak smile and turned to go.

'Excuse me, sir.' Rymer turned back. 'Why did you want to know? You thought a friend of yours was here, perhaps?'

'No, not a friend – but someone. Impossible, of course. The cinema was empty.'

'Well …,' Raúl paused. 'It wasn't empty exactly.'

'Oh? How do you mean?'

'A theatre group were using it. Foreigners. I don't know them, but their driver is a friend of mine.'

'What are they doing here?' asked Rymer.

'*Were*, sir, not *are*. They left for the capital today. They wanted to use the cinema to rehearse* a play* they are going to perform* there. At an Arts Festival, I believe.'

'I see. Do you know the name of the group?'

The man thought for a moment. '*Triangle*, I think. Yes, that's it. There are only three people in the group, you see – plus Juan, the driver. They specialise in plays with few parts*, like the one they are doing at the Arts Festival.'

'I don't suppose you know what it's called?'

'Yes, I do. It's called …' The man looked down to admire his flowery shirt: '… *A Well-Dressed Man*.'

Chapter 7
The Girl on the Night Train

'Eliot?'

'Yeah,' answered a sleepy voice.

'It's Rymer. I just wanted you to know I'll be away for a couple of days. I'm going to the capital.'

'Oh? Why's that?'

'I think I've found out something important. I can't tell you about it now – I'm waiting for a taxi to the station. There's a train leaving at midnight. It arrives at eight o'clock tomorrow morning. I'll phone you then and tell you the news.'

'I can hardly wait. But listen, before you go. We finally found out what the capsule contained.'

'Tell me.'

'Glycerine.'

'What?' Rymer couldn't believe he had heard properly.

'Glycerine. It's used in the production of medicines.'

'Yes, I know that. It's harmless[*].'

'Totally.'

'That means the capsule had nothing to do with the man's death. It doesn't make sense. Why did Aguado go to so much trouble to steal it?'

'Who knows. That's something you could think about on the train.'

'I think I'd rather sleep. Anyway, I must go. The taxi's here.'

■ ■ ■

Rymer arrived at the station just in time. He bought a ticket for a sleeping compartment, numbered 16B, and

He looked towards the middle of the carriage. A girl was standing in the window.

ran down the main stairs. The train was standing at the platform*. The sleeping compartments were at the back. A guard was standing by an open door, looking at his watch. Rymer slowed down and looked at the windows of the last carriage*. The blinds* on most of them were down: the people inside were either sleeping or getting ready for bed. All except one, he noticed. He looked towards the middle of the carriage. A girl was standing in the window.

He knew immediately who it was. It was the red-haired girl he had seen earlier that morning in *Los Pinos*. The girl saw him. This time she didn't turn away but stood there, looking shocked. Suddenly, a hand reached up from her left and pulled the blind down, hard. Seconds later the light went out. Rymer stopped. The expression on the girl's face had been strange. She looked as if she wanted to tell him something.

The guard blew his whistle*, interrupting Rymer's thoughts. He got on the train, showed his ticket and was told that 16B was in the last carriage, the same carriage as the red-haired girl.

He walked along a narrow passage*. There was a crash as a door closed behind him; the scream of metal as the train began to move. And then he heard something else – the sound of someone crying. It came from halfway along the carriage, to his left – the red-haired girl's compartment. He paused. There were no windows on this side of the compartment, but he noted the number on the door: 14B, two away from his own. Puzzled*, he moved on.

He reached 16B and turned on the light. The compartment contained a bed, a long seat opposite, and a small table which pulled out from beneath the window. Next to the seat was another door which led into a small bathroom. He unpacked* his case, took a shower and got ready for bed. He felt tired. It had been a long day. He turned off the light, sat on the bed and pulled down the blinds.

For the second time that day he found himself thinking about the red-haired girl. This time she wasn't alone. But she looked just as unhappy. What else had he seen in her face? She looked intelligent, foreign, a stranger to the city. But above all it was a very expressive face. It had the power to show clearly the emotions of the person beneath. If he had to guess what kind of work she did, one word, above all, came to mind: actor*.

Was it possible that the red-haired girl was a member of the theatre group on her way to the Arts Festival? If the murdered man had been an actor in the same group it would explain a lot of things. It would explain why the girl was in the area where the dead man was found, for instance. And the dead man's clothes: specially made for the play as suggested by its name, *A Well-Dressed Man*. An actor who is involved in a rehearsal doesn't need to carry any form of identity. He works with people he knows. Friends. But in this case one of them was not a friend. One of them had decided to kill him.

Of course, many things were still unexplained. The shoes, for example: actors don't normally take their shoes off to rehearse. And the capsule. If it contained only glycerine, why was it considered so important? And what about the rest of the group? Did they all decide to kill him? That was unlikely. If they were all involved, there would be no need to employ Aguado. So if only one of the group was responsible, what about the others? Why had they not contacted the police?

But there were no others in the group, were there, he suddenly realised. Triangle. Three people: the murdered man, the red-haired girl and the person she was with, the third member of the group – the director? Was that person the murderer? And were they both involved in the crime? Possibly, although the girl wasn't behaving in a guilty way. He remembered how sad she had looked the first time he saw her, and then again from the window of the train. So if she wasn't guilty, that could mean only one thing: that she was being forced into the situation because she was frightened. This would make her difficult to work with, which is why the murderer employed Aguado. Rymer felt sorry for the girl. She had probably never felt more frightened in her life. That was not surprising, if the person she was with was a murderer. A murderer who, if Rymer was right about all this, was lying only a few metres away from where he sat.

He lay back and listened to the sound of the train, racing through the night. Were all these ideas of his fantastic? Who knows? There was only one way to find out. He would check on the people in compartment 14B before they left the train. But not now - in the morning. All would be discovered in the morning.

Rymer closed his eyes. Within seconds he was fast asleep.

──── Chapter 8 ────
Waiting in the Capital

When Rymer woke he knew something was wrong. The train wasn't moving and someone was calling through the door of his compartment. It was the guard, telling him they had arrived. He looked at his watch. It was ten past eight. He had overslept*.

He got up and threw cold water over his face. He dressed quickly, packed* his things and left the compartment. He hurried back to 14B. The door stood open. He looked inside. As he expected, the compartment was empty. He left the train and looked up and down the platform. There was no sign of the red-haired girl or her mysterious companion. Disappointed, he went to the tourist office, booked a room in one of the central hotels and went to look for a taxi.

It was a little after nine o'clock when he arrived at the hotel. A pretty female receptionist told him that she was sorry, but his room would not be ready before midday. Perhaps, she suggested, the gentleman would like to take a walk around the centre? Rymer said he would – after breakfast. She gave him a map of the city and directed him to the hotel cafeteria. He thanked her, left his case at reception and was about to walk away when he noticed a pile of leaflets* on top of the desk. He picked one up. The words *Arts Festival* were written on the front. Underneath, it said that information about the events was given inside. He put the leaflet in his pocket and went for breakfast.

The only people in the cafeteria, apart from the waitress, were a group of businessmen sitting in a cloud

He ordered toast and coffee, sat at a table well away from them and opened the leaflet.

of cigarette smoke. He ordered toast and coffee, sat at a table well away from them and opened the leaflet.

His eyes immediately caught the name Triangle. They were to perform *A Well-Dressed Man* in the *Imperial Theatre* at eight-thirty p.m. on Thursday night, May 2nd. He was surprised when he read the name of the main actor, Miguel Suarez. Suarez was not a member of Triangle, but one of the country's most popular actors. He read on. At the bottom of the page, he saw the words, 'Suarez appears by special invitation'. And then he understood. Triangle had offered Suarez the main part in the play as a sign of respect to the country holding the event.

No other information was given. Rymer put the leaflet back in his pocket and looked at his watch. Nine thirty a.m. The play was two whole days away. He felt impatient. What could he do in all that time? He could phone Eliot, he thought, realising that he had promised to call his friend earlier. But after that? Could he really stay here that long? He would have to. Because he was now certain that the play held the key to the mystery.

Now there was nothing to do but wait.

■ ■ ■

'This passage leads to the main dressing-room', Katrina. Notice the door at the end of the passage. It can be locked from this side. That's good. When Rymer comes to see us I'll lock the door behind him. No one else will be able to get into the area. The three of us will be alone in … here.'

As the final word was spoken a door to the right of the passage was thrown open. On the other side was the main dressing-room. Katrina walked into the room. Behind her, the voice went on:

'The only difficulty will be in removing the body.'

Katrina turned. 'Why do you have to kill him?' she asked.

The reply was quick, as if the question was expected. 'Because he is the only person who can catch us. No one else has either the time, the energy, or the intelligence. And I know him. I know what he's like. He's curious, and honest. Both these qualities are dangerous for us. The first means he will not be happy until he finds out what really happened on Sunday night; the second means he will tell the police. Do you want to spend the rest of your life in prison? I think not. We would be separated forever. And my life is not worth living without you, Katrina. Remember that.'

Katrina said nothing. She felt two hands pushing down on her shoulders. She sat down. Her chair faced the dressing-room door. In front of the chair was a table. There was a bag on the table. She watched in fear as a small object was pulled from the bag and placed in front of her.

Katrina looked up. Two mad eyes stared* back at her.

'And now Katrina, I will tell you exactly what you have to do ...'

Chapter 9
A Well-Dressed Man

On Thursday evening, at exactly eight-fifteen, Rymer arrived at the Imperial Theatre. He had bought a ticket the previous day. He had asked for a seat near the front, the last one in the third row*. From there, he would have a good view of the actors. Also, if the play was boring, he would be able to leave without disturbing* anybody else.

As he walked into the theatre he was given a programme. He went to his seat, opened the programme and saw, to his disappointment, that Triangle would not be appearing until after the interval, at around 10 o'clock. Before that time a group of musicians would be performing 'traditional' songs. He decided to escape while there was still time. He left his seat and went to the bar. He would return during the interval.

The bar was on the first floor. On his way up the stairs a voice announced that the performance was about to begin. Soon, people were hurrying past him, on their way down. He stepped aside and watched them go. What was he expecting? To see the red-haired girl again? The honest answer was 'no'. Maybe he was wrong about her. She was probably just a lonely tourist having problems with her boyfriend. By now they had probably caught a plane back to their own country.

The bar was empty. He sat down in a corner and began to read the programme in more detail. There was information about both Triangle and the play they were performing. Originally European, the group now lived and worked in South America. *A Well-Dressed Man* was written by Paul Czerny, one of the members of the group. There were only two characters in the play, a man called Leonardo, and a woman, Katrina. Leonardo - normally played by Czerny - was tonight played by Miguel Suarez, and Katrina by ... herself? Must be, no other name was given.

There was no information about who the director was. Never mind. He would find out soon enough.

The interval arrived. As the bar began to fill, Rymer went back to his seat in the theatre. He waited. At five to ten people started coming back in. By ten o'clock everyone had taken their seats. A small orchestra played a romantic tune. This was followed by complete silence as everyone looked towards the front of the theatre.

The curtains lifted.

One person stood alone in the centre of the stage*. It was the girl with red hair - Katrina. So, Rymer had been right after all. He tried not to think about what this meant and to concentrate on the play. Both actors were good and he soon became involved in the story:

It takes place in Paraguay, in 1935, at the end of the war with Bolivia. Leonardo, a young officer, returns home after the fighting. Katrina, the only child of German parents and the girl he is to marry, is waiting for him. Her father was killed in the war and she now lives with her mother, a sick and difficult woman who expects her daughter to do everything for her. Katrina looks forward to Leonardo's visit: both because she loves him and because their marriage will help her escape from the situation.

COLD FEET

Now his shoes are no more than a symbol of war. He pulls them off and throws them across the room.

Leonardo arrives. He and Katrina sit at a table opposite each other. He asks for wine. She places a bottle of wine and a glass on the table. After filling the glass she begins to talk about their future together. She is relaxed and happy, but Leonardo seems tense. She asks him about his experiences during the fighting. As he begins to speak, there is the sound of footsteps above their heads. It is Katrina's mother, nervously walking up and down the floor of her bedroom. It soon becomes clear that she is doing this for two reasons: to bother Leonardo, and to make Katrina feel guilty. She is frightened of being left alone and doesn't want her daughter to marry.

As Leonardo talks of the brutal experience of war, the footsteps seem to get faster, and louder. The effect is to increase the power of his story. But they do something to Leonardo, too. They remind him of marching men, the sound of distant guns. Soon the terrible things he has seen fill his mind. He drinks the rest of the wine from the bottle, then, unable to speak, looks down at his own feet. He notices that, in his hurry to see Katrina, he forgot to change his shoes. He is wearing the ones he wore as a soldier. Now they are no more than a symbol of war. He pulls them off and throws them across the room.

At that point in the play Katrina left the stage. A light followed her. Everyone watched - everyone, that is, except Rymer whose eyes were still on Leonardo, sitting in half-darkness. He saw the actor pull something from the top pocket of his jacket, turn away from the audience and lift a hand to his eye. When Katrina returned, a few seconds later, Leonardo was crying.

Rymer had seen enough. He had the solution to the murder. Now he needed to be alone, to organise his thoughts and decide what to do. Quietly, he left his seat and went back to the bar. He sat down and considered carefully what he had just discovered.

The answer to the mystery was in the play. The dead man was Paul Czerny, the man who wrote it. The capsule, known as a 'glycerine tear', is used by actors to produce tears when the glycerine inside is put in the eye. The capsule was not important because it was used to kill the man: it was important because it gave a clue to his profession. That was a clue which Rymer had missed. It was the wine which had contained the drugs - wine which the girl didn't drink, but which, during rehearsal, the victim did. Rymer imagined Czerny feeling strange almost immediately and in an attempt to feel better, leaving the cinema by the side exit. He probably half-fell out into the street and went to sit on the steps of the consulate. A while later, he was dead. A clever murder. And who was guilty? Katrina? – the person who had given him the wine? He didn't think so. It was more likely to be the person who, before the rehearsal, had opened the bottle of wine. And who was that? It could only be one person: the third member of the group, the one whose footsteps he had heard during the performance – the director.

There was applause in the distance – the play had finished. Rymer returned to the theatre. When everyone had left he jumped onto the stage and went behind the curtains. A young boy was taking furniture away. Rymer said he was an English theatre agent and asked if it would be possible to speak to the director of Triangle. The boy asked him to wait and disappeared through a doorway at the back of the stage.

Five minutes later he came back carrying a note. It was short and polite:

> I am busy right now, but I will be happy to see you in the main dressing-room at twelve o'clock.
>
> Thank you
>
> I. Noskov.

Rymer put the note in his pocket. Noskov? The name didn't mean anything to him. He looked at his watch, it was twenty to twelve. Twenty minutes to wait. It was too late to go back to the bar so he helped the young boy to clear away the rest of the furniture. When they had finished the boy thanked him and left. Rymer was about to check his watch again when a sudden movement caught his attention. He looked over towards the doorway at the back of the stage. A man's face looked back at him, then disappeared.

He had only seen the face for a moment; yet in the back of his mind Rymer knew that he had seen it before. But he had no time to remember where, or when. From somewhere in the distance he heard the sound of a clock. It was midnight.

■ ■ ■

The theatre was empty as Rymer walked behind stage. He entered an enormous room full of false walls and strange machines. At its far end a red sign identified the door leading to the dressing rooms. He pushed open the door. On the other side was a long, narrow passage. It was dark except for a single line of yellow light which he thought must come from the main dressing room. He walked down the passage. Halfway along he felt a soft movement of air, followed by a sharp, metallic* sound as if someone had closed a door, quietly, behind him. He stopped, and for the first time felt afraid. Bravely, he walked on.

He reached the main dressing-room and paused outside the door, listening. No sound came from the other side.

Slowly, he pushed open the door.

Katrina sat at a table facing him.
Rymer was about to speak when the lights went out.

Katrina sat at a table facing him.

Chapter 10
A Voice in the Dressing-Room

'Don't move - or you're dead.' Rymer froze. It was a man's voice, slow and deep, coming from somewhere in front of him. He thought of a face, the face of the man in the doorway at the back of the stage. And now Rymer remembered where he had seen that face before. It was the face of the unfriendly man, the one he had met in the hotel bar early on the morning of the murder. Early - that one word reminded him of something Mrs. Strelski had said about getting up early because she was not able to sleep, 'The slightest sound wakes me: a passing car, the cry of a bird, a distant telephone.' Of course. Why hadn't he thought of it before? The man's hotel room was next to his own. He had heard one side of Rymer's conversation with Eliot, enough to know what was happening and to make him contact Aguado.

The voice went on: *'Congratulations, Mr. Rymer. Your hard work has earned you the answer to a mystery, part of which you know already. Part, that is, but not all ...'*

Wait a minute. There was something strange about that voice. Something not quite right. What was it?

'Do you still not know who I am? Come, Mr. Rymer, you know me well.'

At that point a soft, low light, somewhere behind him was turned on. Once again he saw Katrina. His attention was caught by one of her arms, reaching towards a black object lying on the table in front of her. It was a tape recorder. And this, he now saw, was where the voice was coming from.

So is that why it sounded strange? Partly, but there was

something more, something unnatural, and yet almost recognisable about the way the words were spoken. He watched as Katrina laid a hand on the table and began turning something at the side of the machine. Slowly, the voice went higher. '*I hope you have appreciated my sense of humour, Mr. Rymer.*'

His blood turned cold. Now he knew what was strange. It wasn't the voice of a man at all, but a woman. A woman he knew well. The tape was turned off and someone standing behind him said, 'Put your hands on your head, Mr. Rymer. And turn around.'

He turned to face the owner of the voice.

It was Mrs. Strelski.

■ ■ ■

How easily she had deceived him. Of course her profession helped: any actor experienced in using theatrical make-up* is capable of appearing a lot older than they really are. But she hadn't been able to hide everything; for although she appeared younger, she looked just as unhealthy and the two hands holding the gun shook badly.

'So, we meet again, Mr. Rymer. My name, as you know by now, is Noskov, not Strelski, but the Imra is the same.' She pushed the gun towards him. 'Now, there is a chair to your left. Please sit down, slowly. And keep your hands on your head.'

He did as he was told. He had to, the gun was pointed at his heart and he knew she would use it. He couldn't think of any way of stopping her. The chair he now sat in was in the middle of the room. If he tried to move, she would shoot him dead before he could escape. His

He did as he was told. He had to, the gun was pointed at his heart and he knew she would use it.

only chance was to keep Imra talking by asking questions. If she became involved in the answers, she might get careless, careless enough for him to kick the gun from her hands. It wasn't much to hope for.

'Why did you kill Paul Czerny?' he asked.

'I didn't. Katrina did.'

Rymer looked towards the girl. She hadn't moved. She was still sitting with her eyes frozen on the door.

'It was an accident,' Imra went on. 'Katrina fell in love with Czerny. He told her that he loved her too, and said they could get married at the end of the year. But he was lying. He didn't love her at all. He already had a girlfriend, in Argentina. But this girl's family were very poor. Czerny was only marrying Katrina to get her money. He planned to divorce her and then go and live with the other girl.'

'How did you know all this?' asked Rymer.

'I was suspicious. Letters used to arrive for him at the places in which we were performing. One day, while he was out, I took some of the letters from his room. I read them and put them back before he returned.

'I wanted to tell Katrina but I knew she wouldn't believe me. I couldn't prove that what I said was true. Until last week, when another letter arrived. I wanted to steal this last letter and show it to Katrina. But Czerny was suspicious of me and kept it in his jacket pocket. I knew I would need help if I wanted to take the letter. So I spoke to Katrina. I told her that if she read the letter she would find out the truth about Paul Czerny. Of course, she wanted to ask him about it, directly. But I told her not to. He would say that I was trying to cause trouble between them. I knew that the only way to read the letter was to take it while he was asleep. But it would have to be a deep sleep – Czerny was someone who woke up easily. So I suggested using a drug, which we could give him in ... secret.' She stressed the word, then paused to look at Katrina. The girl still hadn't moved.

Imra continued: 'The best opportunity for doing all this was late last Sunday night, during our final rehearsal of the play, when Czerny was going to drink the glass of wine Katrina gave him. So, before we started, she put the drug in the wine. Later, he drank the glass of wine, as we planned. What we didn't know, unfortunately, was how extremely sensitive he was to the drug. At the end of the rehearsal he left the stage without saying anything, and without his shoes. We thought he had gone to bed. He was staying in the cinema that night, in a small room at the back of the building – the owner is a close friend of Juan Soriano, our driver.'

So, thought Rymer, Soriano was the unfriendly man he had seen in the hotel bar, and then again at the back of the stage. 'Was Soriano staying there, too?' he asked.

'No. He always sleeps in the vehicle. I sent him onto the capital early the following day. He doesn't know what's happened. I told him that Czerny had gone back home because his mother was sick. He believes me. After all, Czerny wasn't performing in the capital – Miguel Suarez was.'

'How fortunate,' said Rymer.

Imra Noskov smiled. 'Anyway,' she continued, 'we waited until we thought Czerny would be asleep before going to his room to get the letter. But when we got there, the room was empty. We were disappointed, but not worried. That came later, when Czerny was found lying at the top of the consulate steps. By that time he was dead.

'I knew that if the police found out they wouldn't believe it was an accident. They would arrest Katrina for murder. She would spend the rest of her life in prison. I couldn't let that happen.'

'So is that why you employed Aguado? To stop anyone finding out what happened?'

'No. I didn't want to employ Aguado. But you see, we weren't the first to discover Czerny's body. There was a man standing over him when we arrived. It was Aguado. Katrina was so upset when she found out that Czerny was dead that she told Aguado what had happened. He saw his chance to make money. He spoke to me alone and said that he would help me to cover up the accident if I paid him. If I didn't, he would tell the police. Of course I had to agree.'

'And he stayed with you that night?'

'He didn't trust us. He thought we would leave the city. So he insisted on staying in our hotel room, room 203, the one next to yours. Katrina was feeling very bad, so I had to give her something to help her sleep. But I was unable to sleep myself. I had to sit up half the night listening to Aguado telling me how clever he was. Eventually, I went to the bathroom just to get away from him. When I was alone I began to feel more and more curious about what would happen when Czerny's body was discovered. I looked at my watch. It was almost seven o'clock. I thought of going down to reception. It's the best place to be if you want to find out the latest news – Luis is usually the first person to know if anything unusual happens. But I didn't want to be recognised. So I decided to make myself look older. While I was putting on the make-up, I heard a phone ring - the bed in your room must lie just the other side of the bathroom wall. I heard the word 'murder', put my ears to the wall and heard you speaking with your friend from the consulate. It was enough. I went back into the bedroom and sent Aguado to check on the situation. The rest you know.'

'About the capsule, yes. But you took a lot of trouble over nothing. I'm not as clever as you seem to think. It wasn't until I saw the play that I realised that the contents of the capsule are used in theatrical make-up. What I still don't know is how Aguado was able to get into my room.'

'He went down the stairs without being seen and waited in the bar. You came down and left your key on the reception desk - Luis was in the restaurant at the time, helping himself to coffee. Aguado took the key and followed you. He hid in *Calle Alta* and saw you find the capsule. He then phoned the hotel and told me what had happened. I told him that the capsule was an important clue, it would give you a connection between the dead man and the theatre group. So Aguado decided to get the capsule back. He didn't think this would be too difficult. He still had your key. He could get into your room, hide behind the door and attack you when you walked in - which is what happened, eventually. Anyway, he returned to the hotel and, using your key, opened the door to room 201. There was no time for him to return the key to reception, so he asked me to do it. That wasn't so easy. There was an unpleasant moment when you arrived at the reception desk before I'd had a chance to put the key back. I had to think of a reason to send you away before you found out it was missing. So I said I was upset by news of the murder and asked you to fetch me a glass of water. While you were gone, I replaced the key.'

Rymer shook his head, admiring Imra's intelligence. He knew the answer to his next question but he asked it all the same. 'Later that day you went to Aguado's house and shot him. Why? Did he ask for more money?'

'Yes. He had taken our passports, so we couldn't leave the country before I had given him what he wanted. Later that morning, I took a taxi to his house and paid him what we had agreed. But then, when I asked for the passports he wouldn't give them back and demanded more money. I thought something like that might happen, so I had come prepared. I opened my bag as if I was going to pay him and suggested that we drink to the conclusion of our business. As he was filling two glasses with whisky, I pulled out the gun and shot him. The taxi was waiting for me around the corner. The driver didn't hear a thing.'

Imra had come to the end of her story. 'You're a very clever woman, Mrs. Noskov.' Rymer said. He looked up, sadly. 'You have made me look quite stupid – except for one thing.'

'Oh? What's that?'

'Most of what you have told me is a lie. Czerny's death was no accident. The level of barbiturates in his blood was too high for that. It was murder: cold-blooded* murder. And Katrina wasn't responsible. It was you. And I think I know why.'

'Don't waste words.' Imra's voice was suddenly loud and sharp. 'You're just trying to save yourself. It won't work.'

A VOICE IN THE DRESSING-ROOM

'As he was filling two glasses with whisky, I pulled out the gun and shot him.'

Rymer took no notice. 'It was all in the play wasn't it? The play that Czerny wrote. About a sick and difficult woman who couldn't stand the thought of losing her daughter. You were clever, Imra, but you were too sophisticated. Even when you played the part of Mrs. Strelski you over-acted*. When we were talking, you made an analogy between life and the rising and setting of the sun. It showed me your deepest fear - the fear of loneliness in old age. That fear is greater than the 'love' you feel for your daughter.' Rymer emphasised the word 'love' and looked at Imra, hard. 'But it's not love you feel for Katrina is it? It can't be. If you love someone you want to protect their happiness, not destroy it. Czerny had no other lover, did he? It was a lie. He realised the power you held over your daughter and wrote a play about it. A play which showed Katrina the truth about her relationship with you, and which made you very angry. Angry enough to kill him.'

'Shut up!' Imra screamed. Her face was red, her eyes wild. She held the gun towards Rymer and took a step forward.

But she was still too far away. Rymer knew he wouldn't be able to reach the gun before she shot him. He tried to think of something else to say. But the words wouldn't come. There was nothing more he could do. He closed his eyes, waiting for the end.

'You have nothing to fear, Mr. Rymer. The gun is empty.'

Rymer opened his eyes in surprise. It was Katrina. She had spoken for the first time.

'The bullets* are here,' she said, 'in my hand.' She

opened her hand, dropped six bullets onto the table and began to walk towards her mother.

Imra Noskov moved back and stared at her daughter. 'You stupid girl,' she breathed. 'What have you done?'

'I didn't need Mr. Rymer to tell me the truth about Paul's death, Mother. I found out myself, on Monday afternoon.' She turned to Rymer. 'The letter that was supposed to have been in Paul's pocket. My mother showed it to me. I was suspicious. It looked familiar. On Monday afternoon, while she was having a shower, I took the letter from her suitcase. It was the paper which had made me suspicious. I held it up to the light. The watermark* was a symbol of the city of Rosca. The letter was typed, not in Argentina, but here, by my mother.'

Imra stood against a far wall, her head down. When Katrina spoke again, it was as if she were talking to a frightened child. 'How stupid I've been. For years I've lived in the shadow of a will stronger than my own. Never again. That power is finally broken.'

She took the gun from her mother's hands and threw it into the darkness at the back of the room.

Rymer heard the crash of metal on wood, followed by the sound of Imra, crying. Suddenly, she was an old woman again.

It was the saddest sound he had ever heard.

——— EPILOGUE ———
Sunrise

At six a.m. on the following Saturday morning, Eliot and Rymer were sitting at a table outside *Los Pinos*. They had been up all night, enjoying the celebrations. Most people had now gone home and the square was almost empty once again. Eliot realised that the party was over. He didn't look very happy about what the new day might bring.

'I know what you're thinking,' said Rymer.

'Tell me.'

'You're thinking that I shouldn't have let Katrina and her mother go.' Eliot tried to smile but didn't quite succeed. 'You're thinking,' Rymer went on, 'that although the case is solved, there is no evidence to show who is guilty. The consulate will be considered responsible for what happened and you might lose your job. That's what you're thinking, isn't it? Be honest.'

'Well ...' Eliot paused.

Rymer took a letter and a small card from his coat pocket and laid them on the table. 'You don't need to worry. All the evidence is in there.'

'What is it?' Eliot asked in surprise.

'A murder story. I asked Katrina to write everything down exactly as it happened. She did. Then she got her mother to sign it. All you have to do is show this to the police. Her phone number is on the card if you need to speak to her.'

Eliot picked up the letter but left the card where it was. 'I don't think that will be necessary.' He looked thankful, then puzzled. 'Why didn't you give me this earlier?' he asked.

'I promised Katrina not to show it to anyone until she and her mother had left the country.'

Eliot smiled. 'I understand,' he said, touching Rymer's glass with his own. 'Here's to a man with a soft heart.'

'Cheers,' said Rymer.

They finished their drinks and Eliot stood up to go. 'Don't forget you're having dinner with me tonight.'

'I won't,' said Rymer.

They were silent for a moment, then Eliot asked, 'When are you leaving exactly?'

'Ten o'clock tomorrow morning.'

There was a pause. 'I'll be sorry to see you go,' Eliot said, at last.

'Me, too,' said Rymer. He watched his friend walk away and suddenly felt lonely. But he knew it wasn't only Eliot he would miss.

He picked up Katrina's card. Not now, but at some time in the future, he would call that number. Who knows? She might just give him the best reason in the world for coming back to South America.

Rymer put the card in his pocket but he didn't get up. Instead, he turned to the east and watched the sky, slowly turning red. It was years since he'd seen the sun coming up.

But Imra was right. It was a beautiful sight.

EXERCISES

A Comprehension

Chapter 1 and 2 Write answers to these questions.

1 What was suspicious about the death of the man found outside the consulate?
2 Why did Eliot want Rymer to investigate the man's death?
3 A man was carrying something in his right hand. What was it?
4 What was interesting about the girl Rymer saw in the café window?
5 Why was Mrs Strelski upset?
6 What did Rymer discover after he'd been attacked?

Chapter 3 and 4 Are these sentences true (T) or false (F)?

1 Aguado lived in an expensive part of the city.
2 The postman saw Rymer and went to call the police.
3 Katrina found a letter inside a small black case.
4 Eliot tells Rymer that the capsule contained barbiturates.
5 Rymer thinks that Luis heard his telephone conversation with Eliot.
6 Eliot will tell the police about Aguado's death.

Chapter 5 and 6 Who said these words?

1 'Come and join me.'
2 'You're very kind.'
3 '... a passing car, the cry of a bird, a distant telephone.'
4 '... that cinema is closed on Sundays.'
5 'The cinema was empty.'
6 '...: A Well-Dressed Man.'

Chapter 7 and 8 Who in these chapters...

1 ... tells Rymer what was inside the capsule?
2 ... buys a ticket for compartment 16B?
3 ... is crying on a train?
4 ... suggests a 'walk around the centre'?
5 ... appears by 'special invitation'?
6 ... is pushed into a chair?

Chapter 9 and 10 Answer these questions.

1 In the play, why does Leonardo throw his shoes away?
2 What is a 'glycerine tear'?
3 Who is Juan Soriano?
4 Who was the first person to find Czerny's body?
5 Why did Czerny write the play?
6 How did Katrina find out that her mother was lying?

B Working with Language

1 Match the sentence halves and then check your answers in Chapter 3.

a It was a nice place to live
b He went back to the front door and
c As he looked up
d He put back the wallet
e The footsteps started again,

i then disappeared.
ii a sudden rush of wind closed the door.
iii if you had the money.
iv and turned to search the room.
v stepped inside the house.

2 Complete these sentences with the correct form of the verbs in brackets.

1 And now Rymer remembered where he (see) that face before.
2 If he tried to move, she (shoot) him dead before he could escape.
3 'There was a man standing over him when we (arrive).'
4 'While I was putting on the make-up, I (hear) a phone ring.'
5 'If you love someone you (want) to protect their happiness, not destroy it.'

C Activities

1 After she finds the dead man, Carmen Viguera talks to a newspaper reporter. Write his report about the mystery of the dead man at the American Consulate.

2 Imagine the conversation between Aguado and Imra at Villa Rosa and write a dialogue.

3 Rymer leaves his seat before *A Well-Dressed Man* has finished. Think of an ending to the play and write a summary of it.

GLOSSARY

actor *(n)* a person who performs in plays

banknote *(n)* paper money

blind(s) *(n)* a roll of material for pulling over a window to keep out the light

bullet *(n)* a small metal object that goes inside a gun

carriage *(n)* one of the sections of a train that carries passengers

cleaner *(n)* a person who is employed to clean the inside of a building

clue *(n)* something which gives information that will help solve a problem

cold-blooded *(adj)* without feeling or emotion

develop *(v)* make pictures from a photographic film

disturb *(v)* interrupt and cause inconvenience to someone

dressing-room *(n)* a room in a theatre where actors dress and make-up before a performance

driving permit *(n)* an official document which allows you to drive

employee *(n)* a person who works for you is your *employee*

exit *(n)* a doorway leading out of a building

fatal *(adj)* causing death

harmless *(adj)* something which has no dangerous effects

heels *(n)* the lower back part of the foot

label *(n)* a ticket on an object which gives information about it

leaflet *(n)* a little book or paper containing information about something

loaded *(adj)* a *loaded* gun is a gun with bullets in it

lower *(v)* speak more quietly

over-act *(v)* act too strongly with the result that people don't believe you

overdose *(n)* if someone takes an *overdose*, they take a very high, dangerous quantity of a drug

oversleep *(v)* continue to sleep after you had intended to wake up

pack *(v)* put one's clothes into a suitcase or bag

parts *(n)* characters in a play*

passage *(n)* a long, narrow space with walls on both sides

perform *(v)* do something to entertain other people; *n:* **performance**

phone booth *(n)* a box or kiosk with a public telephone in it

platform *(n)* a place in a station where you get on and off a train

play *(n)* a piece of writing which consists of the words that a set of characters say

poisoning *(n)* dangerous or fatal effect of taking a high quantity of a drug

proud *(adj)* feel pleased or clever about something you've done

puzzled *(adj)* be confused by something you can't understand

rehearse *(v)* practise something in order to get it right; *n:* **rehearsal**

remove *(v)* take away

roof *(n)* a covering on top of a house

row *(n)* a number of people or things arranged in a line

rush *(n)* a sudden increase in strength or speed

scene *(n)* part of a play*

shadows *(n)* dark places on a surface made when light can't reach it

shutters *(n)* metal or wooden covers over windows which stop light getting in

socks *(n)* a piece of clothing which covers the foot and goes inside the shoe

stab *(n)* a sudden, sharp feeling

staff *(n)* all the people that work in a place

stage *(n)* a raised floor in a theatre where people perform*

stare *(v)* look at something for a long time

sunrise *(n)* a word used to describe the sun coming up in the morning

sunset *(n)* a word used to describe the sun going down at the end of the day

teenager *(n)* a young person between the ages of thirteen and nineteen

theatrical make-up *(n)* cosmetics used by actors*

tremble *(v)* shake because you are ill or upset in some way

unpack *(v)* take one's clothes out of a suitcase or bag

watermark *(n)* a mark on paper made by the company who make it and which you can only see by holding the paper up to the light

wooden *(adj)* made out of wood

whistle *(n)* a small metal tube, which you blow into to make a sound